South Union Shaker Village

Photographs and Text by

David Toczko

Foreword by

The Sabbathday Lake Shakers

Acclaim Press
MORLEY, MISSOURI

Acclaim Press
— Your Next Great Book —

P.O. Box 238
Morley, MO 63767
(573) 472-9800
www.acclaimpress.com

Book Design: Tiffany Schaefer
Cover Design: M. Frene Melton

Library of Congress Control Number: 2013923513

ISBN-13: 978-1-938905-50-6
ISBN-10: 1-938905-50-4

First Printing 2014
Printed in the United States of America
10 9 8 7 6 5 4 3 2 1

Contents

Dedication

This book is dedicated to the memory of my mother, Martha Toczko Marshall. It was she who first introduced me to and impressed me with the Shakers and their way of life. The memory of her passion for this time in history has stayed with me all my life.

Acknowledgments

As the saying goes, "No man is an island" and such an undertaking as this book can't be done without the help, advice and input from others. A special thanks goes to the entire staff of South Union Shaker Village. They enthusiastically embraced the idea of this book and were instrumental in making it the publication it has become. Tommy Hines, Executive Director, provided me the access to the most prized possessions in their archive as well as input on the historical significance of the many items contained in this book. Kaelin Vernon, Operations Manager of South Union, provided the historical context and importance of many of the items and architecture that make up South Union. JoAnn Moody, Shaker Tavern Innkeeper, who made my overnight stays comfortable and my breakfasts delicious!

A small, but special, circle of friends also provided moral support, input and advice that was taken to heart and deeply appreciated. To John Snell, Karen Kasey and Wayne Stacy, my heart-felt thanks.

My deepest thanks go out to Beth Roberts. While these may be my images, this book is every bit hers as it is mine. She has spent countless hours going through the thousands of images I took to bring you the best images that best tell the story of South Union. From editing, to layout, to the occasional kick in the butt when things hit a standstill, she has been by my side to make this dream become a reality. No words can express my thanks for all she has done.

The South Union Shaker Village wishes to acknowledge Mrs. Curry Hall, whose strong sense of preservation, love for local history, and Southern gentility paved the way for saving the Shaker legacy at South Union. And to Julia Neal, who committed much of her life preserving South Union through research and the written word, we say thank you. Your efforts are why we are here today.

Foreword

"From Poland's [Maine] bleak heights to South Union's sunny plains," is a line from a hymn composed by Elder Otis Sawyer of the Maine Ministry. Elder Otis was one of only two Maine Shakers to ever have visited South Union during its long and venerable history as a Shaker Community. He was impressed by the lay of the land. The flat fields, fertile soil, majestic buildings, and warm climate remained with him through the rest of his life.

The present-day Maine Shakers completely concur with our venerable Elder. Although our visits have been few, they have always been inspired with a sense of place that feels like home. The warm welcome from Director Tommy Hines and his staff, the beauty that is South Union itself and the spirit of all those consecrated souls whose presence still lingers also still inspires.

The beautiful photographs by David Toczko bring back many memories of our time spent in Kentucky and, more importantly, give us a desire to return — soon!

We send you all greetings from the Shakers' most eastern and northern Community (and only remaining one) to our friends in the most southern and western Community!

Peace.

The Sabbathday Lake Shakers

Introduction

Between 1807 and 1922, a communal religious sect called the Shakers occupied a six thousand acre farm in southern Kentucky. Within the confines of this vast plantation, the group constructed a village that boasted over two hundred buildings, including massive dormitories, subsidiary shops and outbuildings, barns and stables, and a mill complex that was unequaled in the region. The Shakers called their village South Union.

The strict lifestyle of the Shakers involved communal living, celibacy, withdrawal from the "world," and an emphasis on simplicity and perfection in all things. South Union drew a majority of its members from the Upper South, thereby creating a Shaker community with strong regional customs and traditions. A distinctly "Southern Shaker" material culture and folklife were inevitable byproducts, evidenced not only in the community's furniture and architecture, but in the clothes its members wore, what they ate, and how they communicated.

The South Union Shakers were quite successful in their communal experiment, gathering a population of nearly four hundred by the late 1820's, establishing successful industries, and reaching a peak level of economic prosperity prior to the Civil War. During the 19th century, South Union depended upon its farmland for not only sustenance, but for its financial success. Agrarian-based industries that included the sale of pure bred cattle, the production and marketing of brooms, silk, and fruit preserves, and the sale of garden seed, provided a comfortable lifestyle for the community. Modern and efficient factories, workshops, and barns were constructed by the Shakers to house state-of-the-art equipment that helped to insure the success of their business ventures.

Financial hardship caused by the Civil War, followed by declining membership and failing industries throughout the late 19th century, altered forever South Union's state of financial prosperity and spiritual initiative. By 1922, when only nine members remained, the decision was made to close the community and to sell the land, buildings and personal property. A public auction was held in September of that year.

The restoration and historic preservation of South Union began much later, thanks to the efforts of Mrs. Curry Hall and a corps of Auburn, Kentucky volunteers. Her valuable combination of drive and gentility helped amass the beginnings of the South Union collection, displayed to the public for the first time in 1960. By 1972, the organization had purchased two of the original Shaker buildings at South Union and the course was set for future development. Today the South Union Shaker Villages owns and interprets seven of the nine remaining village structures, and protects five hundred acres of the original farm.

David Toczko's wonderful photographs successfully capture the essence of South Union. Its handsome brick buildings, its expansive southern Kentucky landscape, and its finely crafted objects have never looked so good. The Shakers' well-known legacy of craftsmanship is evident throughout the pages of this book.

We must not forget, however, the reason that these buildings, this landscape and these objects have such timeless appeal. The real success of the Shakers can be attributed to their spiritual endeavors. A strong faith and a lifestyle centered on worship created the true legacy. Theirs was a culture of humility, tolerance, equality, artistry, and stewardship. Shaker faith is what produced the tangible things you see in this book.

We at the South Union Shaker Village feel strongly about preserving that legacy, and are humbled by the opportunity to preserve, protect, and interpret the Shakers' most southern outpost.

Tommy Hines
Executive Director
South Union Shaker Village

Elder William Bates (1864-1931) (standing, left) and visitors Harvey McCutchen and G. W. Pottinger, ca.1920. This photograph is thought to have been taken to document one of the later land sales at South Union. Photo courtesy of South Union Shaker Village Library.

While all of these photographs were taken in professional studios, it was common at that time to have traveling photographers stop to take people's portraits. Elder Logan Johns (1842-1924) Photo courtesy of South Union Shaker Village Library.

Eldress Harriet Breedlove. Photo courtesy of Western Reserve Historical Society.

Elder Harvey Eads (1807-1892) Photo courtesy of South Union Shaker Village Library.

Elder James Richardson. Photo courtesy of South Union Shaker Village Library.

The Centre House at South Union. The front of this and many other structures were oriented to face the south. This allowed the Shakers to take advantage of the prevailing west winds for ventilation as well as to maximize natural light throughout the day.

1824

The Centre House now and as it appeared in the 1880's. Construction of the "new" Centre House was begun in 1822 and completed in 1833. The original Centre House was located to the east and adjacent to today's Visitor Center. Photo courtesy South Union Shaker Village Library.

The Centre House at night takes on a totally different feel than that during the day.

The Centre House now and then, ca. 1915 as seen from the Ministry Shop. Photo courtesy of Canterbury Shaker Village Library.

The Centre House decorated for the Christmas season.

An interesting shadow of the railing on the front steps of the Centre House.

Elder John Perryman (1845-1916) poses with visitors from "The World" to South Union, ca. 1910. People who were not members of the Shaker community were referred to as being from "The World". Photo courtesy of South Union Shaker Village Library.

The front of the Centre House as seen from the former location of the Meeting House.

An archival photograph, ca.1885 taken from a similar angle. Photo courtesy of Western Reserve Historical Society.

The front of the Centre House through a second floor window in the Ministry Shop.

Above and right: Various photographs of the front elevation of the Centre House.

The Centre House during the auction of 1922. Photo courtesy of South Union Shaker Village Library.

Right: The front of the Centre House as seen from the Ministry Shop.

1824

The west side elevation of the Centre House in the autumn.

Inset: South Union Shakers and Visitors pose on the east side of the Centre House, ca. 1910. Photo courtesy of South Union Shaker Village Library.

A view through a first floor level window on the west side through to the east side of the Centre House. This is a prime example of how they designed their buildings for natural cross ventilation.

The lattice work of the west side porch creates interesting patterns on this chair. The porch was added shortly after the Civil War to facilitate cooking outdoors during the summer months.

A detail of the door entering the first floor from the west side porch.

Above and right: Various photos of the rear elevation of the Centre House.

East side elevation of the Centre House. The covered well to the right serviced not only the Shakers, but travelers and locals from "The World".

The rising sun is reflected in the windows and lamp posts on the east side of the Centre House.

Right: Windows in the attic of the Centre House not only provided light, but needed ventilation in the summer.

The setting sun peeks through the bell tower of the Centre House.

1824

Background: The east side of the Centre House during the "Golden Hour" at Sunrise.

Inset: South Union has been listed on the National Register of Historic Places since 1974.

Restoration efforts to the east side chimneys done in 1972 are evident in this photograph.

A detail of a gate hasp on the east side of the Centre House.

A boot scraper located outside a door indicates the belief the Shakers held that cleanliness is next to Godliness.

A candle lantern at an entry to the Centre House. The perforations in the lantern allowed light to radiate and reduced the chance of wind blowing out the candle.

The east side entry door to the second floor of the Centre House at sunrise.

The bell tower, located on the roof of the Centre House, was used to call members to meals and in the case of emergencies.

Background: The well shed, built in the 1820's by the Shakers, was shared with the local community and travelers.

Left: The east side door to the first floor of the Centre House shows the years of use and memories of all who passed through it.

Right: One of the many lamp posts at South Union decorated for the Christmas season.

Below: A night time photograph on the east side of the Centre House.

Examples of the utensils the Shakers would have used in the 1900's.

One of the caster sets that was part of the place settings. While they seem ornate to the modern observer, they were very commonplace at the time.

Far right: An example of the way the Shakers set their table in the 1900's. The smaller table at the far end is where the Elders would sit.

The view out one of the south facing windows of the Centre House's first floor.

Examples of some of the containers the Shakers used to store their foodstuffs.

One of the windows in the dining area of the Centre House. The colors are original to the structure and show the Shakers enjoyed using them. This photograph also gives one an idea of the thickness of the exterior walls. The flared window sills were not only aesthetically appealing, but were also practical in that they allowed more light into the room and aided in ventilation.

Above, below and right: Examples of various apple peelers used by the Shakers. They embraced technology and employed it wherever they could. The top photo is an example from the 1800's while the bottom photo is of a 1900's version.

Right: This pail, with its original indigo blue paint, is a prime example of how much the Shakers embraced colors.

Items in the pantry just off the kitchen. This is one of the few rooms that was kept locked because of the valuable items, such as sugar, that were stored there.

The hearth in the kitchen area of the Centre House. The churn pictured is original to South Union.

Left and below: Additional items on display in the pantry..

Above and background: Examples of items used in open fire cooking at South Union. The Shakers abandoned this practice as soon as possible for obvious safety and efficiency reasons. The Centre House was completed in 1833 and by 1840 they had purchased a new stove which was placed in front of the fireplace.

Blackberry
WINE.
FROM
D. C. BRAINARD,
NEW LEBANON, N.Y.

The Shakers of South Union made wine and whiskey for both personal use and for sale.

By using polished reflectors, the light from oil lamps was amplified in the rooms.

Examples of some of the cooking utensils used at the time.

Water was piped into the buildings for washing dishes and drinking. When the Centre House was completed in 1833, it already had running water. This was the case for the dwelling houses and some of the workshops as well. This sink is in its original location and the original drain pipe still runs through the wall to the outside.

This view from the main entrance on the second floor of the Centre House shows the classic symmetry of Shaker design. The dual staircases and doorways speak to the Shaker practice of separation of the sexes with men on one side of the building and women on the other.

Above and right: The signature arches of South Union provide not only beauty, but enhanced structural strength. Also visible are the electrical lights that were added in the early 1900's. All of the doors in the Centre House employed arches over them to enhance the structural integrity of the building. Many were intentionally covered with plaster at the time of construction.

Examples of the second floor entryway in the Centre House featuring the classic dual staircases and signature arched openings. The archival photo includes linoleum runners on the main traffic patterns on the floor and was taken at the time they were preparing to add electrical lighting. Photo courtesy of South Union Shaker Village Library.

An interior view of the front door and sidelights of the Centre House.

A view of the main hallway from the front door of the Centre House.

A detail of one of the front door sidelights of the Centre House.

A classic South Union Shaker rocker in one of the Brothers' bedroom located on the east side of the Centre House. The shape of the finials on the back of Shaker chairs was unique to each village and has helped in identifying their origins over the years. This chair was purchased at the auction of 1922 and has since been returned to South Union by the family.

A detail of a built-in cabinet found in one of the bedrooms. These were used to store folded textiles and other personal items.

Left, far left and below: This Sister's bedroom is decorated with original South Union items as it would have appeared in the Victorian era. The view through the lace curtains is accented by the fall colors outside. The use of curtains was adopted in the late 1870's.

A detail of one of the doorknobs on a cabinet in the hall shows the years of use.

A "Tin Lillie" oil lamp in the Centre House. The metal pipe at the top vented the fumes and soot out of the building through the walls of the structure.

Far left: A detail of the inside of the front door on the Centre House shows the evolution of the locks and doorknobs employed over the years.

A classic South Union rocker and candle stand in a Sister's bedroom on the west side of the Centre House.

A detail of a woman's Victorian style boot. The cobbler was one of the most important members of the community.

A view of the front entryway from the Meeting Room.

The Meeting Room in the Centre House shows the various means of heating employed over the years. Steam heat was added just three years before the community closed.

A view of the Meeting Room from the north. Features such as the "Tin Lillies" and the signature arched hallway are evident.

Various detail photographs of a Sister's bedroom. Featured above is a copy of "The Testimony of Christ's Second Appearing" which was in essence the Shaker Bible.

While the Shakers celebrated Christmas, it was more a day of personal reflection and helping those less fortunate. As time went on, they did decorate and exchange small gifts, but certainly not to the extent we do today.

Time was very important to the Shakers and clocks could be found in most of the buildings. With a population that swelled to nearly 400 members, a set schedule was needed to keep things running smoothly.

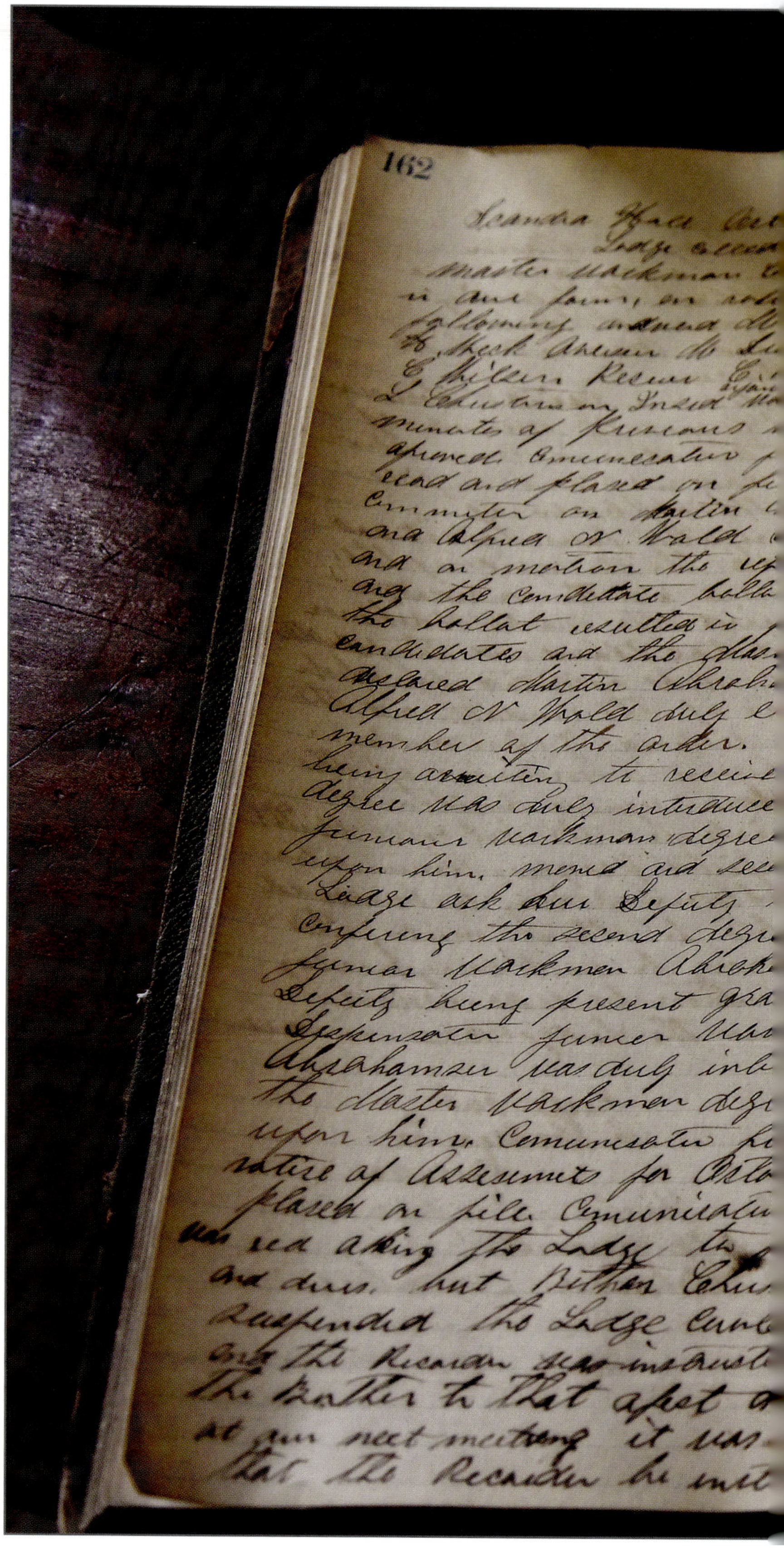

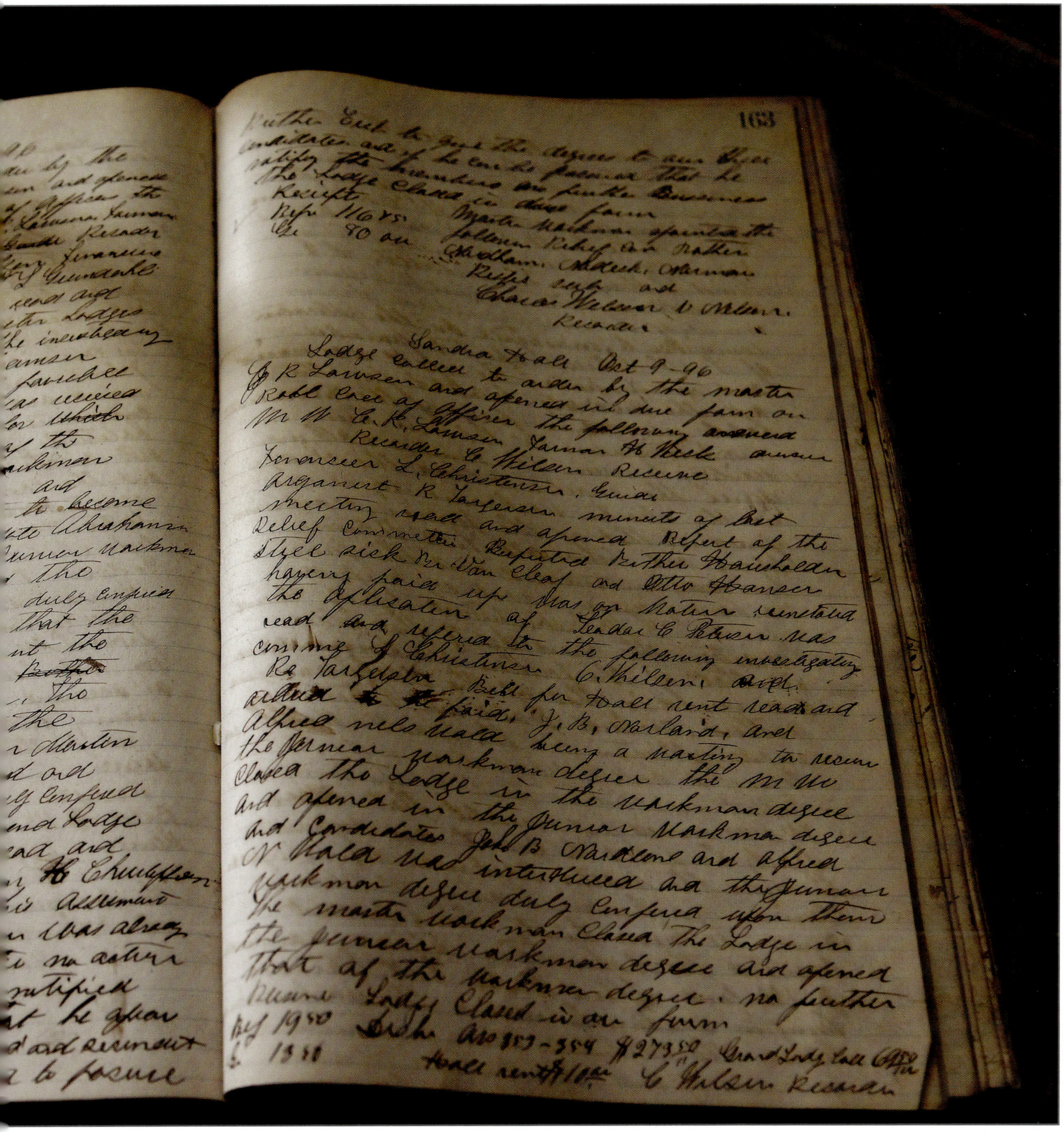

The Shakers were meticulous record keepers, often noting the weather conditions four times a day. Members also maintained personal diaries and journals which provide a wonderful insight into what their lives were like.

Views of the third floor hallway in the Centre House now and then. Photo courtesy of South Union Shaker Village Library.

Details of a Victorian era Sisters' bedroom featuring beds owned by one of the last Shakers of South Union. Depending on the population of the community, as many as four members could have shared a room. Also shown is a stereoscope, a popular device of the time.

Various laundry related items on display. The Shakers adapted this chair for the comfort of the person ironing. The washing machine, interestingly, was powered by gasoline.

A swift, also known as a weasel, was used to measure and keep track of how much yarn was to be used. After 40 revolutions it would make a popping sound to let the person know the prescribed amount had been wound. Popular culture has it this is where the expression "Pop goes the weasel" came from.

The Shakers raised sheep for wool, flax for linen, silk worms for silk and unsuccessfully tried to grow cotton.

This spinning wheel was used for spinning silk, which was produced at South Union.

The Shakers patented many medicinal mixtures. This sarsaparilla syrup, manufactured by the Shakers in New Hampshire, claimed to be a remedy for indigestion, diarrhea and several other ailments.

Shaker style straw hats show how the wooden pegs set into the walls could be used.

A fine example of a South Union miniature chest. Today we would refer to this as a night stand or bachelor's chest.

A bedroom showing the communal nature of their living arrangements. Not much time was spent in the bedrooms other than for sleeping, journal entries and reading before retiring.

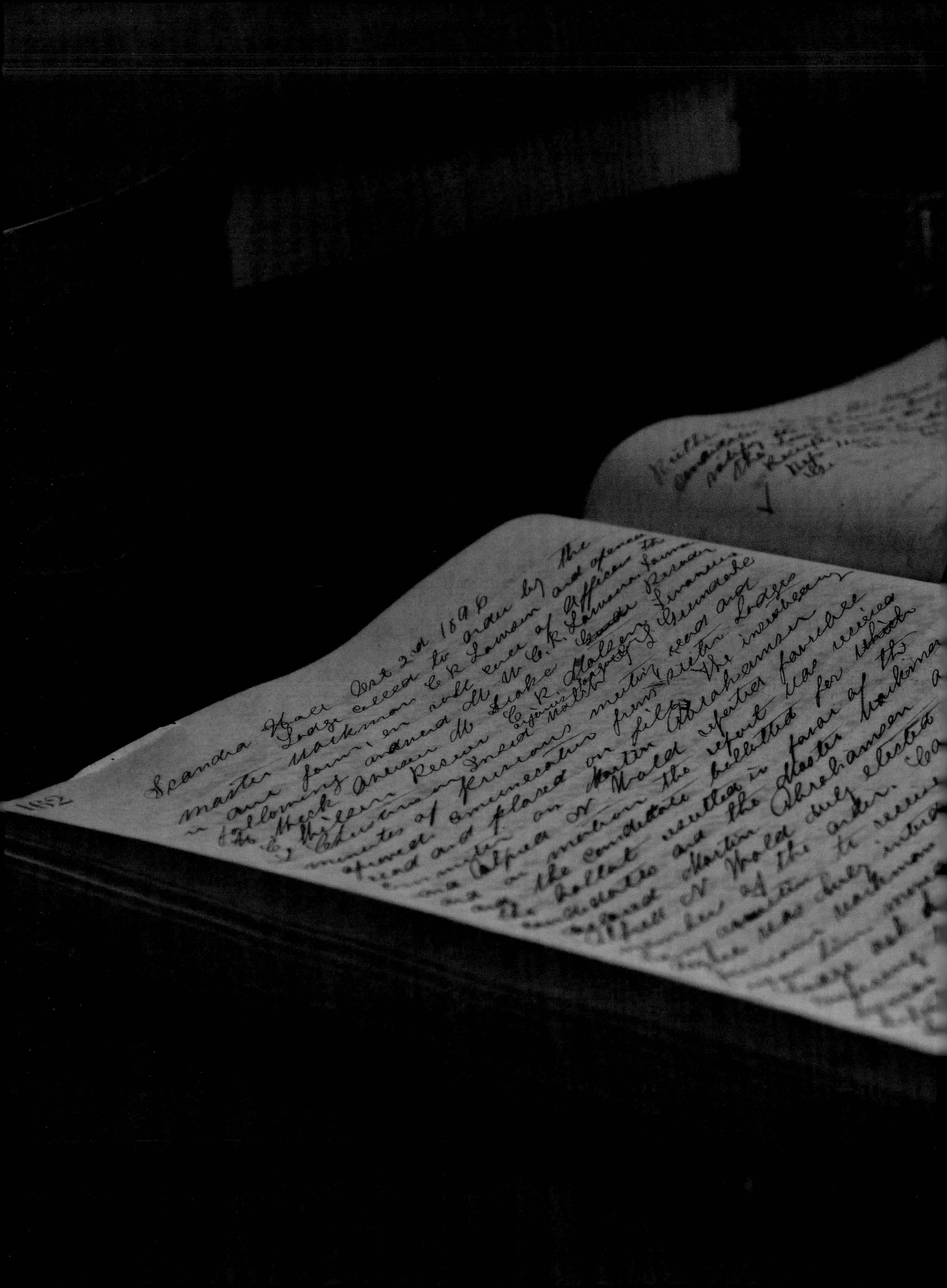

Left: Indoor bathrooms were added to the Centre House in 1916.

Background: Each one of the communal families had their own school as well as a separate dwelling for the younger children. These items are from actual South Union schoolhouses. A South Union wash stand with its original paint can be seen in the foreground.

A Victorian era bedroom featuring a bare bulb electrical fixture. This was a welcome improvement over the kerosene lamps used prior to this addition.

Inset: Detail photo of an 1880's sewing machine.

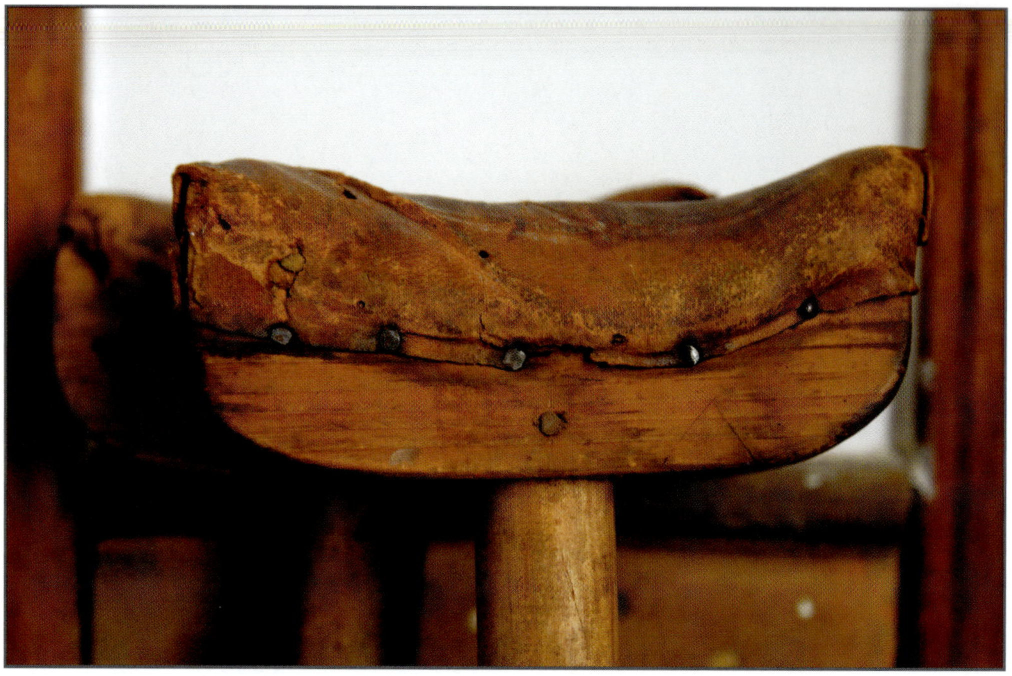

Items from the Infirmary display featuring an adult sized cradle and a mortar and pestle. While not formally trained, nurses who had knowledge of various herbs that could be used for medicinal purposes were assigned to the infirmary and dispensed commercially patented medicines.

ARTHUR PETER & Co.
LOUISVILLE. KY.

Various medicine bottles recovered at South Union during archeological digs. Some bottles recovered from the former Ice House still had medicine in them. Dr. Burr from Auburn made regular visits to the community. Many of the items at South Union were obtained from the Burr family as the Shakers often paid for his services with baskets or furniture.

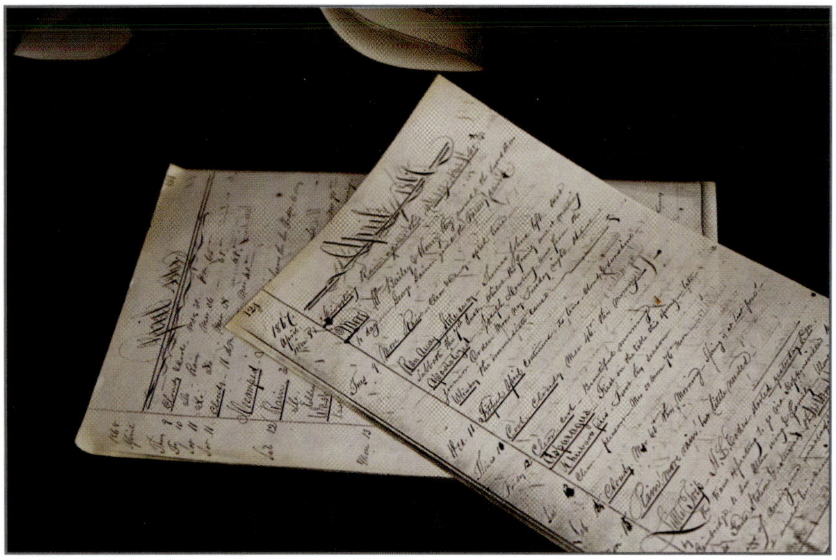

A copy of an April 1867 journal noting weather and other events of the community.

A "Cooling Board" located just outside the Infirmary. This was used to carry the bodies of members who had passed. It is also thought they were placed on this while lying in state.

A patient's bed employing a back board allowed the person to sit upright comfortably in bed.

Right: The nurse's desk used for journal entries and holding reference materials.

Left: A South Union child's chair.

Trunks were stored on the fourth floor of the Centre House. These trunks were used when traveling and also for additional storage of items not frequently used.

A late 19th century Shaker style doll bed in a child's room.

The front windows of the third floor hallway give a mysterious glow to the pedestal placed beneath them.

The only known surviving full seed label box from Kentucky.

5 Cents per Package
PLENDID GARDEN
THE
KERS'
nion, Ky.)
N SEEDS
te of the South than Seeds grown in a colder region.
S OF BOX:
Melon, Montreal Nutmeg.
Banana,
Mustard, Curled.
Brown.
White (Medical.)
Giant Southern Curled.
Okra, Dwarf.
Onion, Large Red.
White Silver Skin.
Parsley, Double, or Curled.
Sugar, or Hollow Crown.
Large Red.
Extra Early.
Early May.
White Marrowfat.
Long Scarlet.
Crimson Turnip Rooted.
White Summer.
Salsify, or Vegetable Oyster.
Spinach, Smooth Seeded.
Early Dutch Bunch.
True Hubbard.
Tomato, Large Red, Livingston's Favorite.
Acme,
Large Trophy.
Summer Turnip, Purple Top, Strap Leaved.
White Top, Strap Leaved.
Purple Top, Ruta Baga.
Flat Dutch.
THE MONEY THAN ANY OTHER COMPANY

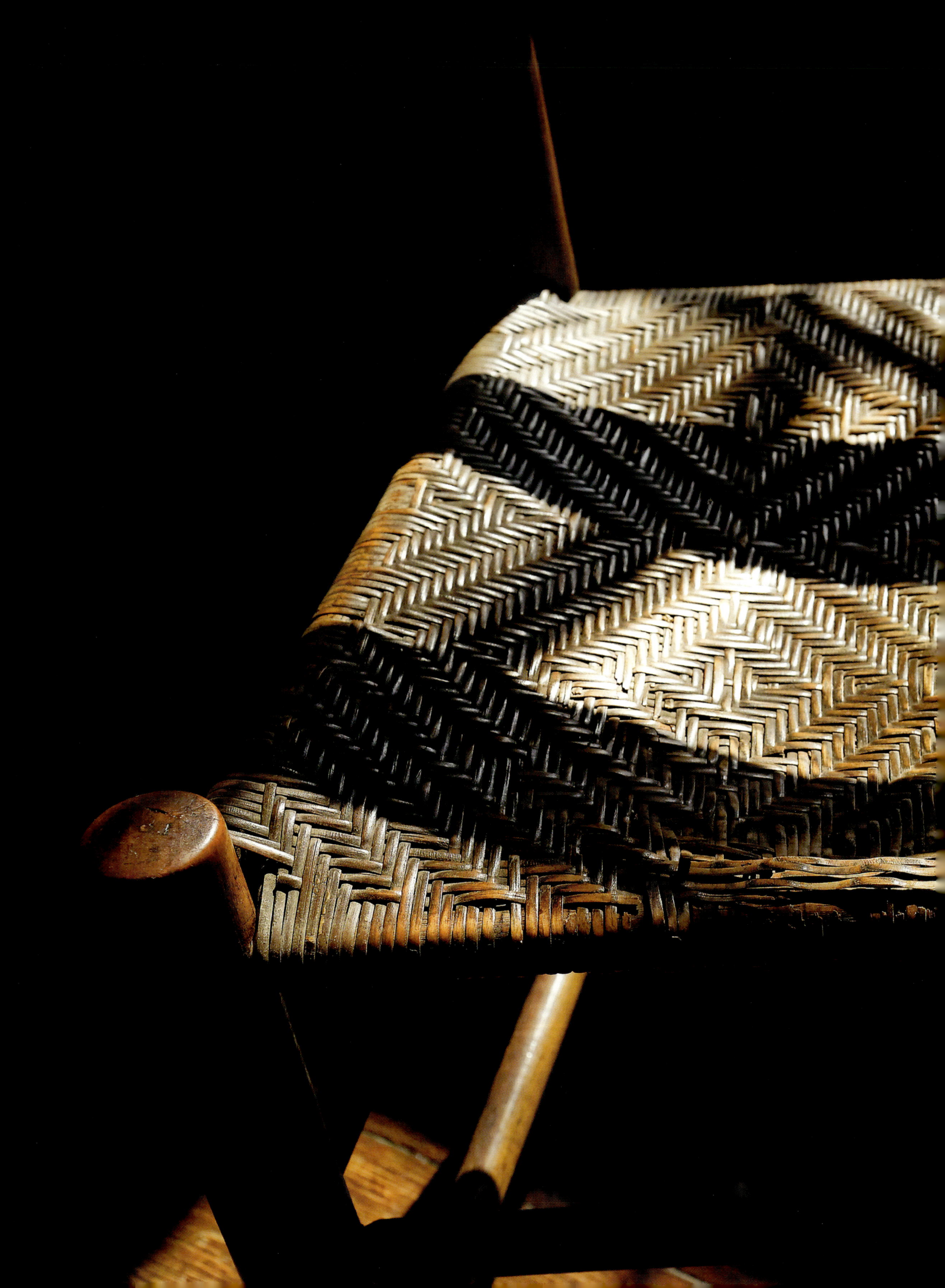

An original South Union chair featuring a Native American pattern in the chair bottom. The white oak baskets were also made at South Union.

An original South Union candle stand.

Original South Union Mochaware again shows how much they enjoyed and used color.

Original South Union white oak baskets made using large wooden molds.

Original South Union silk scarves. The Shakers raised their own silk worms by feeding them mulberries and then spinning the silk for a wide variety of items.

Architectural details of the attic area in the Centre House featuring mortise and tenon construction.

1835
SMOKE &
MILK HOUSE

Various exterior views of the 1835 Smoke and Milk House. This was an auxiliary kitchen where the Shakers made their butter and cheese and cured their meat. Once the curing was done, that portion of the building was locked and used for storage. The Sisters would retrieve meat from there when preparing meals.

Details inside the Milk House portion of the building featuring a churn used by the South Union Shakers. When the crank was moved up and down, it caused the dasher to move in a circular motion.

Broom making was an important commercial aspect of South Union as well as the other Shaker communities. Acres of broom corn were raised to provide material to make the brooms.

Brooms in various stages of construction.

A detail in the downstairs butcher shop in the Smoke House portion of the building.

Various metal kettles on display in the upstairs curing area of the Smoke House.

A classic Shaker cabinet in the butcher shop area featuring the ochre color that was so popular at South Union.

A basket was hung from the heart shaped handle of this pot and was used as a deep fryer.

Hams and sausage were hung from the rafters while being cured and also when stored for future use.

A view from the upstairs curing room of the Smoke House.

Although a bit disorienting, this photo of the Sister's Privy is a reflection outside one of the rear windows in the Smoke House. Cedar trees were planted to provide additional privacy for the Sisters.

The 1854 Wash House now and then. This building was used not only for laundry, but for pressing, mending and other textile related activities. In later years, there was a music room used to teach singing to members and apartments where several Sisters who worked in the laundry lived. Photo courtesy of The Filson Historical Society.

Exterior views of the Smoke House and Wash House from the east.

The mound cistern to the east of the Wash House. The self contained structure was fed by downspouts from nearby buildings. The water from this cistern was pumped back out by a horse drawn mechanism for use in the Wash House. The opening in the end was cut after the Shakers auctioned the property in 1922.

In 1916 a group of
South Union. Recently
was a photo album
House and the Ministry

The view featuring the remains of the Meeting House foundation as seen from the third floor window of the Centre House. The archival photo, ca. 1915, shows the Meeting House as it was originally. While meeting houses were prescribed to be wooden and painted white, the scarcity of timber in the region precluded the use of brick. Photo courtesy of Canterbury Shaker Village Library.

Views of the Meeting House and Centre House now and then. Photo courtesy of Western Reserve Historical Society.

Remains of the Meeting House foundation featuring the dual steps, one set for the men and one for the women.

The 1846 Ministry Shop now and then. The gentleman on the steps appears in several archival photos and is thought to be William Bates who escorted the photographer around the property. Photo courtesy of Canterbury Shaker Village Library.

The Ministry Shop where the Elders and Eldresses lived and worked.

The remains of the Meeting House foundation are reflected in a window of the Ministry Shop.

Exterior views of the Ministry Shop.

One of the bedrooms in the Ministry Shop featuring the original chrome yellow colored floors.

"Shaker Theology", a book written by South Union member and scholar Elder Harvey Eads.

Exterior views of the 1846 Ministry Shop, the second of which was built at South Union.

The fence along the front of the Ministry Shop has an indentation to allow members, as well as passersby on this main thoroughfare, to view the sundial located on the other side of the fence.

The sundial in the front yard of the Ministry Shop was a useful tool for both the Shakers and people of "The World". The original sundial that stood there is now on display in a museum in New York.

The sundial in the front yard of the Ministries' Workshop was a useful tool for both the Shakers and people of "The World". The original sundial that stood there is now on display in a museum in New York.

Views of the staircase in the Ministry Shop featuring all accurate colors of the time.

An original South Union rocker is featured on the Eldresses' side of the Ministry Shop.

Phone service was installed in 1876, the same year it was developed by Alexander Graham Bell, and exemplifies the Shaker's fervor to embrace technology. While not connected to the outside world, the Shakers had a system that allowed them to communicate between buildings in the community. This phone connected the Ministry Shop to the Trustees' Office.

Above and below: Items in the office of Elder Harvey Eads.

Right: Elder Harvey Eads' desk in the Ministry Shop.

persuasion
standard-b
notice
assemblage in the
course was
during which
found and resp
bly. Among
ing him on
intelligent

who had the privilege of hear-
of the State. It
influential men
all an able, and by many an
argument in support of Pedobaptist
Neither Mr. V—— nor any one in
appeared in defence of the course which
the positions he had taken.

Details of items that would have been found in the Loom House that was part of the original community.

The upper floor of the barn was used to store grains. The windows were used for ventilation and the wainscoting was an attempt to keep mice out of the grain.

The platform scales were used to measure grain yields as well as to conduct business. Neighboring farmers also brought their grain wagons here to be weighed.

An exterior view of the barn restored to its original colors. The windows did not contain glass to aid in ventilation as did the louvers in both ends of the barn.

The only post-Shaker barn built by the new owner, Oscar Bond, remaining on the property.

Located next to the Bond barn is a collection of bricks, stone pavers, lintels and various other Shaker building materials recovered from the property over the years and used in the restoration efforts.

A close up view of the Bond barn shows years of weathering since its construction in the 1920's.

Details of the ruins of the cow barn built in 1919 and located on the north side of the property. Oscar Bond demolished the barn in 1930 and constructed another on the same spot. The ruins are a mixture of the two barns which stood there.

The mound cistern adjacent to the cow barn which would have had vegetation over it at the time it was utilized.

Various views of the 1847 Steam House adjacent to the 1919 cow barn. The Shakers developed and patented a process to produce a heated mash they could feed to their cattle in the winter. It is supposed to have made their cattle fatter and glossier but was very expensive to produce and the Shakers abandoned the practice after about a dozen years.

This sign tells of one of the saddest chapters in South Union's history. With the help of a grant and the services of the University of Kentucky Archaeological Department, the boundaries of the six acre cemetery containing 425 graves were identified.

A single marker, modeled after the one at the Sabbathday Lake Community, was dedicated on April 16, 2011.

The sun sets behind the single cemetery marker at South Union.

The Shaker Tavern, built in 1869, was a commercial venture by the Shakers to produce additional revenue. Taking advantage of the railroad that passed through the property, the Shakers built and leased this and other buildings to people of "The World" to run as commercial ventures. The term "tavern" at the time had a meaning more like today's bed and breakfast rather than a bar.

The metal rods that run through the outside columns also run through the building and were used to stabilize the structure due to its close proximity to the railroad tracks.

Below and left: The Shaker Tavern as it appeared in 1922 and today. The railroad was both a blessing and a curse for the Shakers. While it provided a convenient and economical way to transport goods, the rail lines were of major importance to both the Union and Confederate armies during the Civil War. Several skirmishes for control of the railroad took place in the area and both armies used it as a route to move troops north and south. It is estimated the war cost the Shakers in excess of $100,000 at the time in confiscated crops, livestock and material by both forces. Photo courtesy of South Union Shaker Village Library.

The general store as it appeared in 1917 and now. Located next to the Shaker Tavern, this was another commercial building constructed and leased by the Shakers. This building last served as a post office until its closing in 1992 and is currently unoccupied. This area was designated a National Historic District in 1975. Photo courtesy of South Union Shaker Village Library.

Left: The Shaker Tavern plaque.

Next spread: A view of the staircase in the Shaker Tavern from the second floor. The ornate décor and furnishings were meant to attract guests who were traveling via the railroad. This was rather successful monetarily for the Shakers and although several people leased the property, it was an ongoing venture until it was purchased at the 1922 auction and converted into a private residence.

Various interior photographs of the Tavern show the stark difference between the Shakers' way of life and that of "The World". The Tavern now operates as a bed and breakfast once again.

Part of the original dam that powered the various mills located at the west end of the property on the Clear Fork of the Gasper River. Originally the mills were powered by the stream's flow and later by steam generated from its water. The tree which has taken root in the walls today is an analogy for the Shaker's determination to survive and succeed. Photo courtesy of South Union Shaker Village Library.

The Gasper Meeting House was a focal point of the religious revival in Kentucky from 1797 to 1805. Not only was it the birthplace of the Cumberland Presbyterian faith, it also served as a springboard for the formation of the Shaker community at South Union in 1807. Elder Rankin was preacher of this church at the time of the Great Awakening under the preaching of James McGready and objected to the course pursued by the revivalist. Afterward, he founded the Society of Shakers at South Union and was for many years the driving force behind the Society living to nearly 100 years old.

A view from a north window on the third floor of the Centre House. The remains of the 1919 cow barn are visible in the background.

Inset: A view from inside the circle of trees where special services were held.

Background: The Holy Ground at South Union. In the 1840's and 1850's the Shakers held outdoor worship services inside this circle of trees that was the highest elevation of the property.

Leicester Longwool Sheep were first introduced to America by George Washington and Thomas Jefferson as a way to improve the stock here. Only 491 of these sheep exist in the U.S. today and a total of 2,500 worldwide. Part of the mission of South Union, as well as other Shaker communities, is the preservation of endangered breeds of animals.

A view of the Centre House from the cemetery at South Union.

Various images of the new marker erected at the cemetery of South Union.

Index